LEONEL MOURA

BEBOT

ASTANA

PARIS

LISBOA

BeBot was made in cooperation with the company BEHIND (ESI Group) to perform at the 2017 Astana World Expo and subsequently at Grand Palais in 2018 and Gulbenkian in 2019.

15 robots were produced which are fully operational.

Leonel Moura

BEBOT edition, 2019

Cover:

050517, 2017, permanent ink on canvas PVC, 280 x 470 cm

Fondation Guy and Myriam Ullens Collection

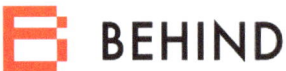

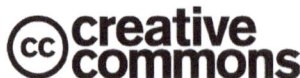

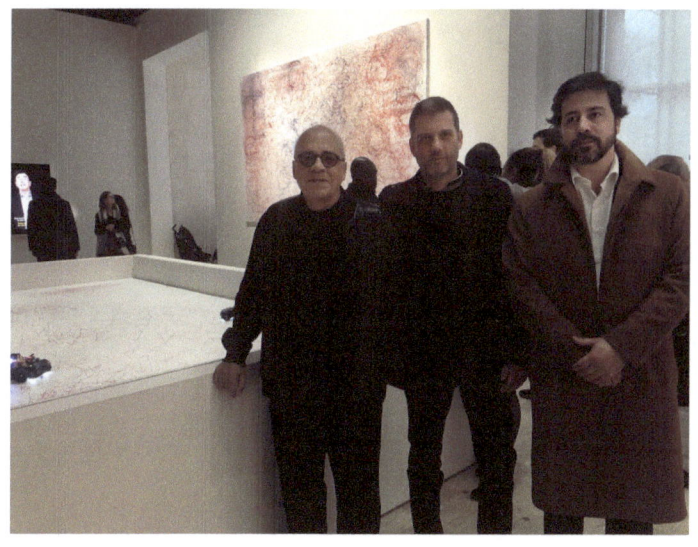

With Gil Sousa and Luís Leitão from ESI Group at Grand Palais, 2018.

BEBOT, 2017, is a Swarm of Art Robots able to collectively invest the canvas to generate unique paintings[1].

These painting robots are artificial 'organisms' that create their own art forms. They are equipped with environmental awareness and a small brain that runs algorithms based on simple rules. The resulting paintings are not predetermined, emerging rather from the combined effects of randomness and stigmergy, that is, indirect communication trough the environment.

As opposed to 'traditional' artworks, the constructing of the painting by the collective set of robots can be followed step-by-step by the viewer. Hence, successive phases of the art-making process can be differentiated.

Although these robots are autonomous they depend on a symbiotic relationship with human partners. Not only in terms of starting and ending the procedure, but also and more deeply in the fact that the final configuration of each

---

1 The first Swarm of painting robots, coined ArtSBot, was created in 2003. http://www.leonelmoura.com/artsbot-2/

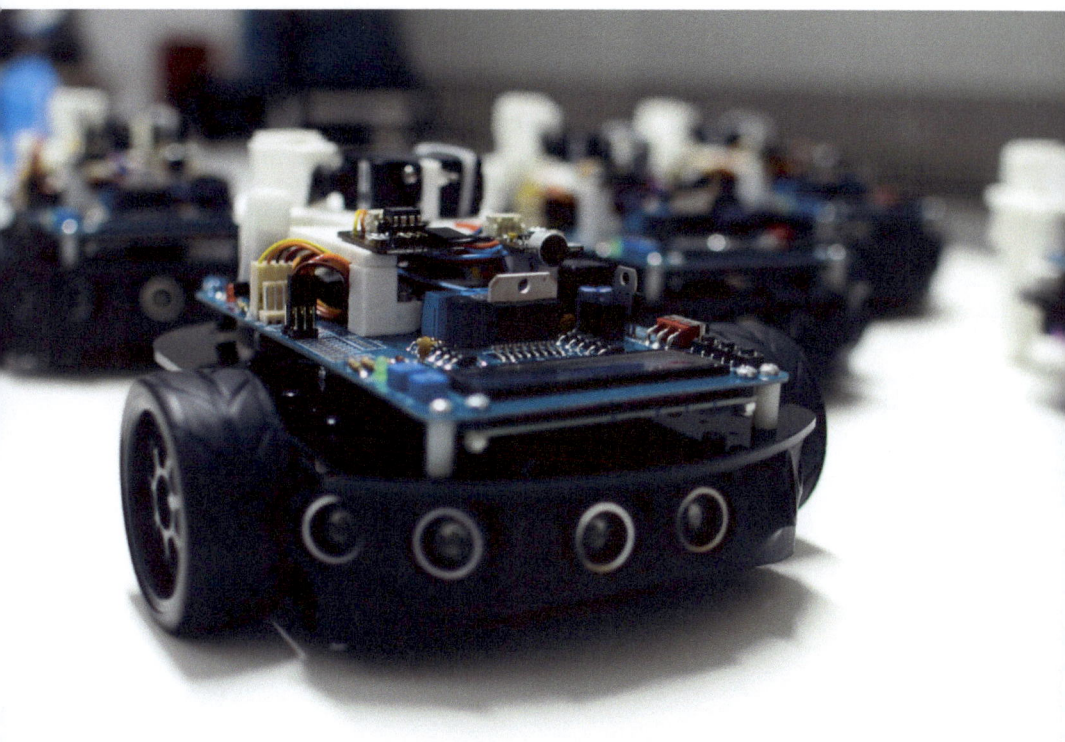

painting is the result of a certain gestalt fired in the brain of the human viewer. Therefore what we can consider 'art' here, is the result of multiple agents, some human, some artificial, immerged in a chaotic process where no one is in control and whose output is impossible to determine. Such a 'new kind of art' represents the introduction of the complexity paradigm in the cultural and artistic realm.

A swarm of autonomous robots able to produce their own art based on simple rules, randomness and stigmergy opens for the human viewer the opportunity to understand life and aesthetics beyond the anthropocentric paradigm and the mystifying separations it generates.

If robots can make art, humans can envision a global consciousness based on co-operative and distributed creativity, with no distinction between human beings, other life forms and machines.

ASTANA
JUNE | SEPTEMBER | 2017

CONTEMPORARY ART CENTER

Artists & Robots

June 10 – September 10, 2017 Astana Contemporary Art Center (ACAC), Astana, Kazakhstan

This exhibition is jointly organized by the Meeting of National Museums – Grand Palais
and "Astana EXPO-2017".

Rmn – Grand Palais selected as artistic component of the Astana International Exhibition 2017. The international exhibition "Astana EXPO-2017", held in the capital of Kazakhstan from June 10 to September 10, 2017 on the theme " FUTURE ENERGY ", invites visitors to reflect on the importance of this vital issue for humanity, thus determining the economic and social development of present and future generations. The Astana Contemporary Art Center of Expo Astana 2017, located at the heart of the international exhibition site, will host, alongside the Garage Garage contemporary art museum, the Rmn-Grand Palais, which presents in preview, an exhibition on the imagination called "Artists & Robots", organized by Miguel Chevalier and Jérôme Neutres. This initiative is part of Rmn – Grand Palais' international development strategy and reinforces its position as a leading cultural player in Europe.

This is the first stage of the exhibition "Artists & Robots". It will then be presented at the Grand Palais in Paris from March to July 2018 in an enlarged version before traveling to other countries.

Artists and robots: rules of artificial imagination?

Our world has been transformed universally and consistently by advances in artificial intelligence and its scientific, industrial, financial and domestic applications. We could therefore forgive ourselves for thinking that art, to paraphrase André Malraux, would be the last (direct) way from man to man. The Artists & Robots project explores this other aspect of the rule of advanced technology, less known but equally real: the advent of the artificial imagination. Is a machine able to be equal to an artist? Can a robot ever replace a painter or a sculptor? To what extent is there artificial creativity? Five hundred years ago, Leonardo da Vinci designed dream machines: a floating palace, a helicopter, a tank, an industrial loom. But this kind of visionary genius does not seem to have dared to imagine a machine to replace the artist. Machines to create: these are the works presented in the first museum exhibition organized by the Rmn-Grand Palais to deepen the artificial imagination in its different artistic materializations and to answer the major challenges of this technical revolution: the artists creators of machines who create art.

The exhibition presents seventeen art installations made between 1980 and 2017, all generated by software. These robots were designed, programmed and installed by artists from thirteen countries whose works are part of museum collections around the world. All the creations presented in this exhibition – paintings, sculptures, mobiles, immersive installations, architecture, design and music – are the fruit of a collaboration between the artists and the robotic programs that they invented. These computer programs are not only intelligent, they are also creative, as they are able to produce unprecedented shapes and figures that give us something to look at and think about.

Artists: Memo Akten, Jacopo Baboni Schilingi, Michel Bret and Edmond Couchot, Miguel Chevalier, Demian Conrad (Automaton), Elias Crespin, Michael Hansmeyer, Raquel Kogan, Peter Kogler, Lab[au] (Laboratory of Architecture and Town Planning), Sonia Laugier and François Brument (In-inflections), Rafael Lozano-Hemmer, Leonel Moura, Nervous System, Quayola, Stelarc, Patrick Tresset.

Curators: Miguel Chevalier, artist, and Jérôme Neutres, director of strategy and development of the RMN-Grand Palais

Exhibition montage Voxels Productions: Nicolas Gaudelet, Emily Lesne, Sam Twidale, Antoine Villeret

A film by Claude Mossessian

Video shoot: Claude Mossessian and Thomas Granovsky

in PRESS RELEASE RMN

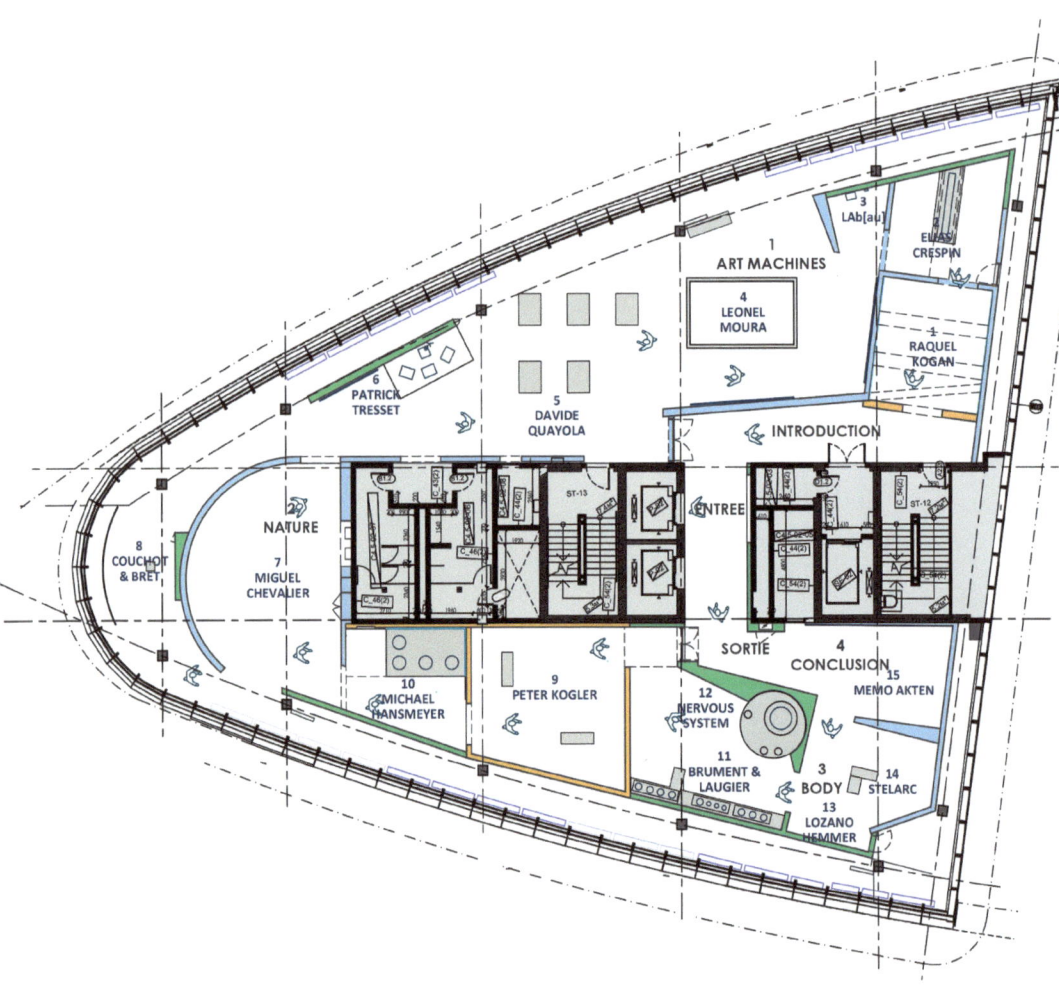

Exhibition plan

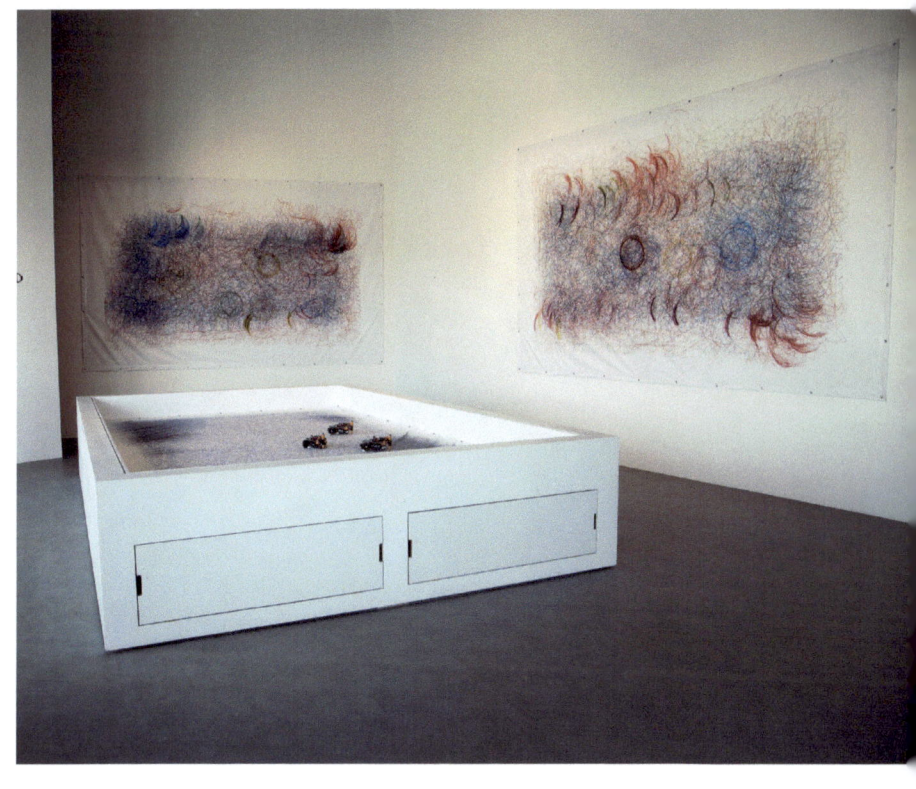

Bebot installation. Photo Thomas Granovsky

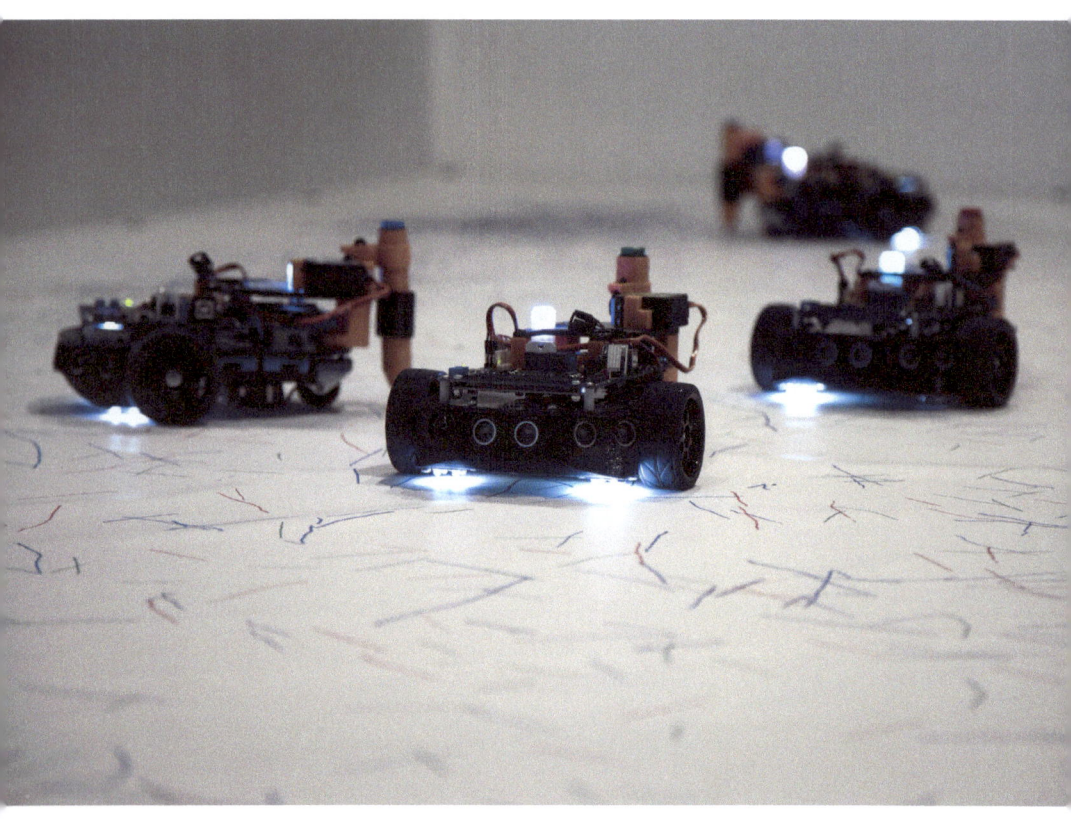

Bebot robots. Photo Thomas Granovsky

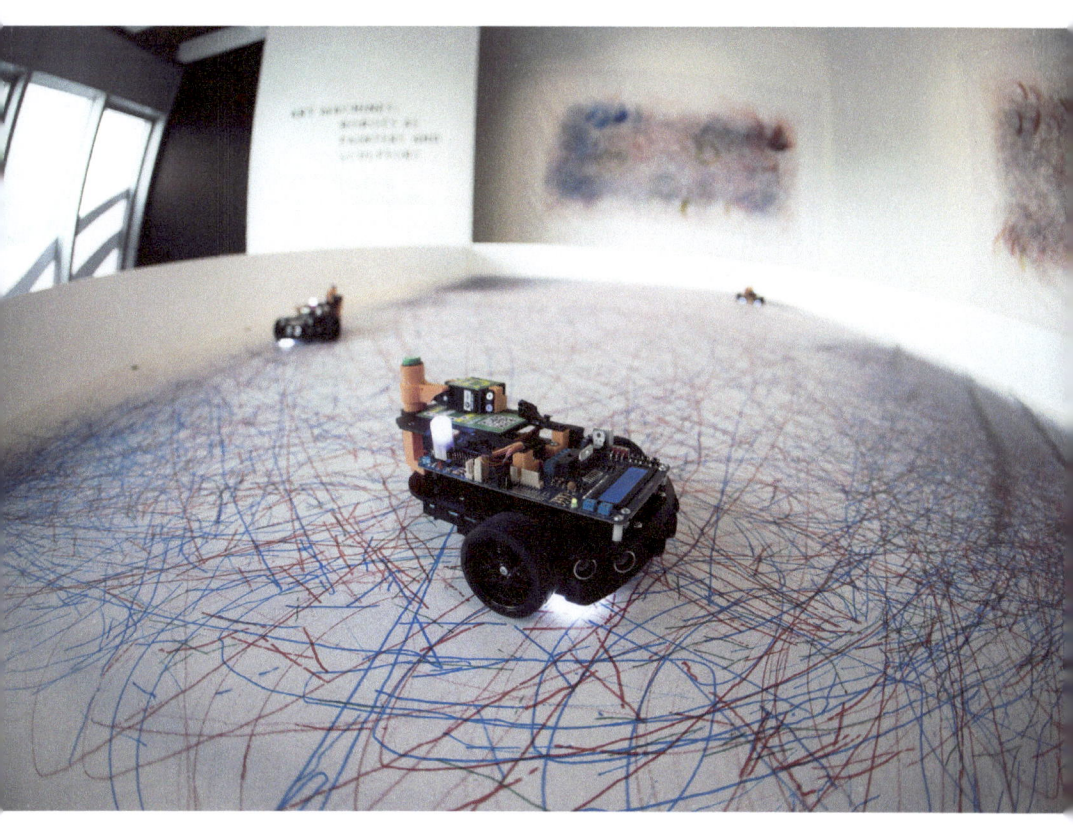

Working. Photo Thomas Granovsky

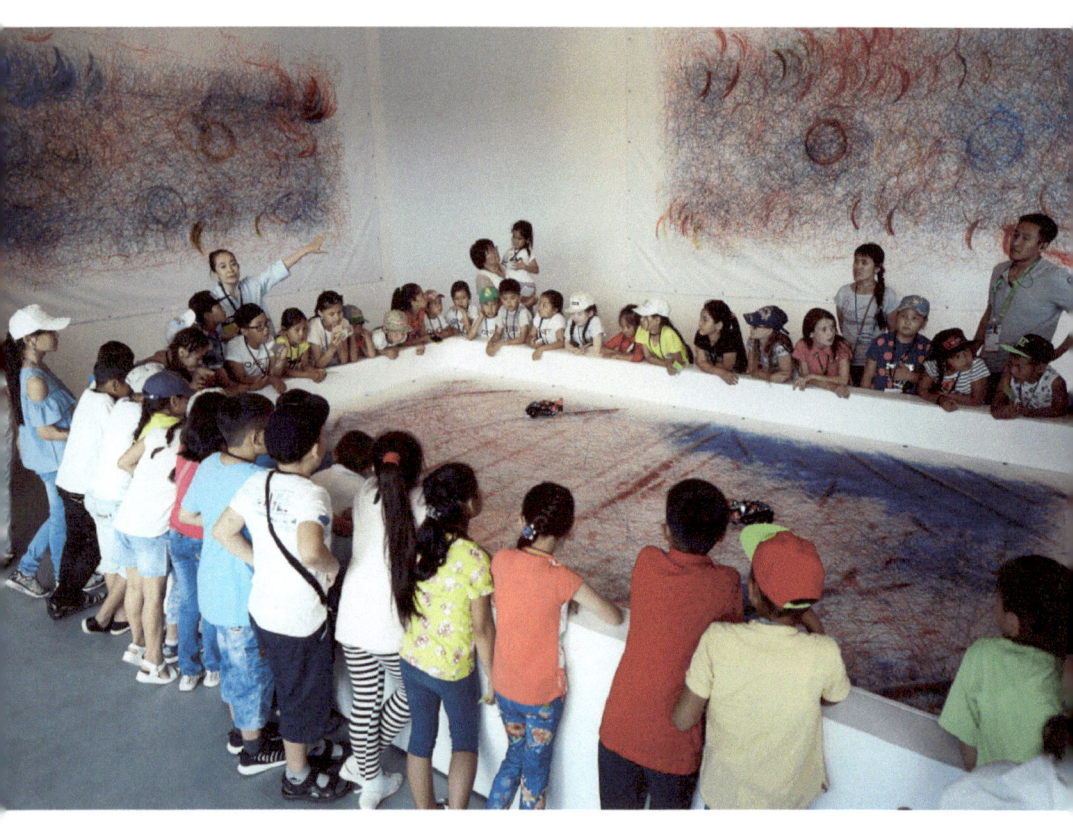

Kazakh kids visiting the show.

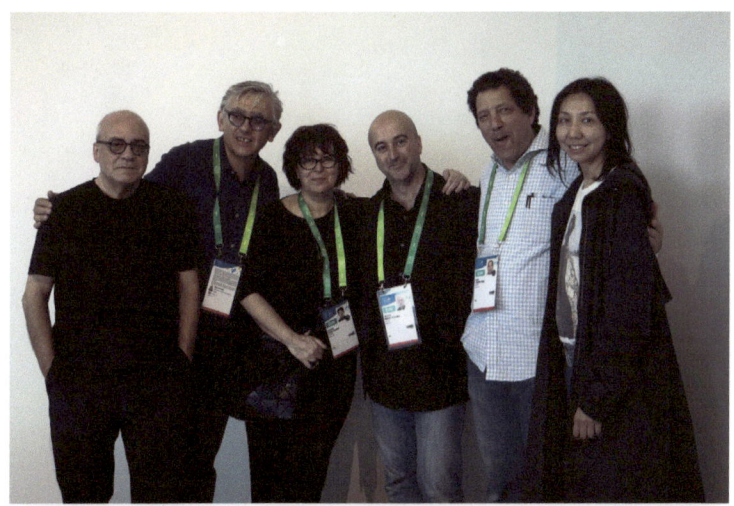

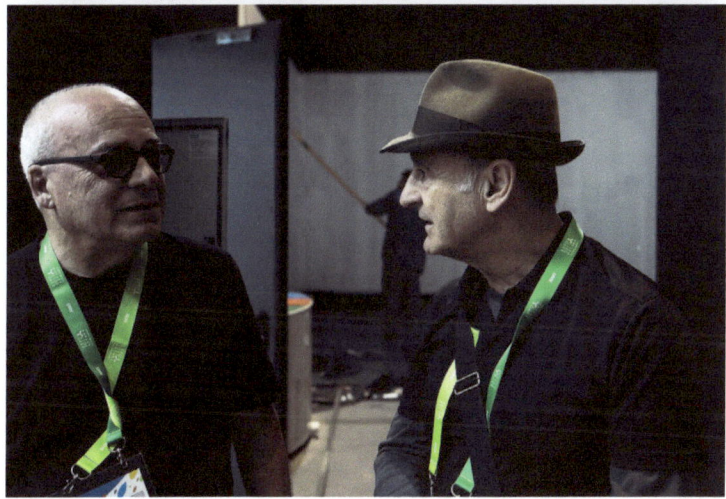

Above: with friends Miguel Chevalier, Raquel Kogan, Jacopo Baboni Schilingi, Elias Crespin and Jama Nurkalieva.
Under: with Stelarc
Photos Thomas Granovsky

This is our first exhibit, it is called "The Art of Robots". You can see that these are the machines and each of them is equipped with a chip with an algorithm that is constantly evolving. Each robot has a sensor in the front, which prevents them from colliding with each other. When they approach each other, they receive a signal and drift apart. Their program modifies at that moment. Therefore, each time they draw different paintings, you can see on our walls. It takes 4-5 days for them to draw one painting. All paintings are abstract, in the spirit of modern art. There is a great field for the imagination; therefore each viewer can attach absolutely any meaning to a painting.

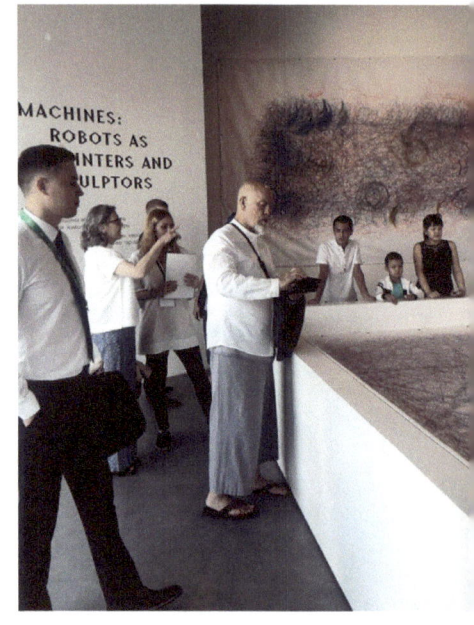

John Malkovich visiting the show

SANIYA BAZHENEYEVA

[Contemporary Art Center]

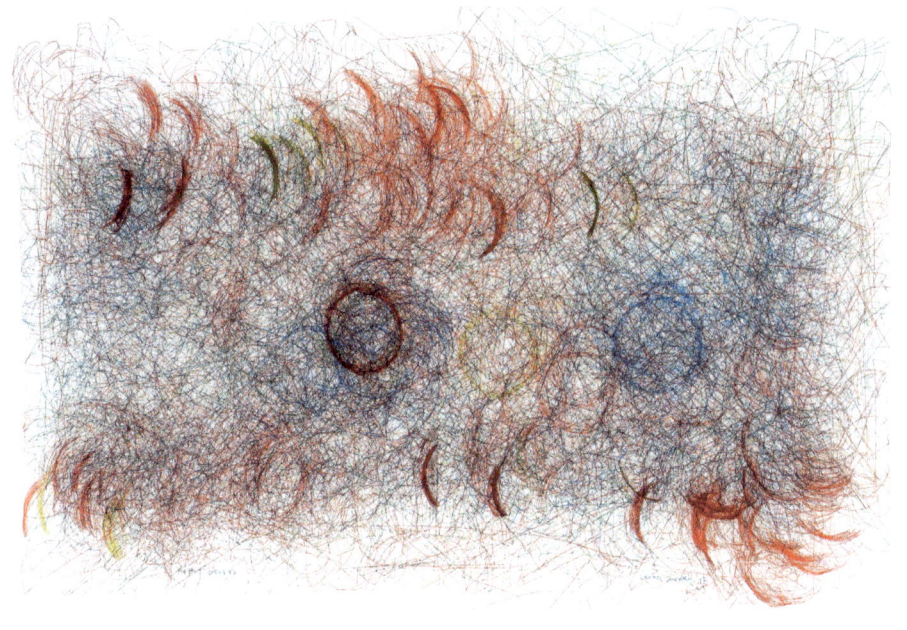

050517, 2017, permanent ink on canvas PVC, 280 x 470 cm.

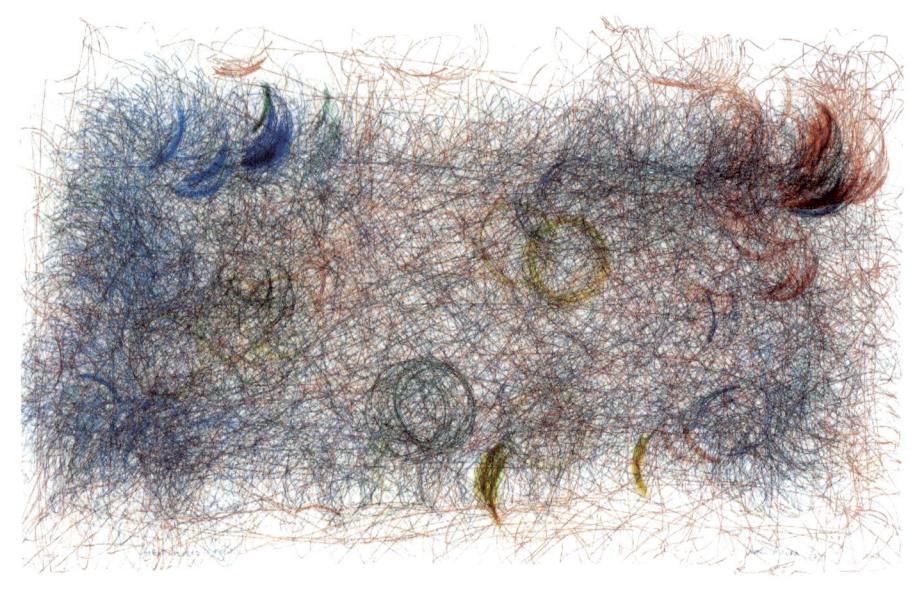

020517, 2017, permanent ink on canvas PVC, 280 x 470 cm

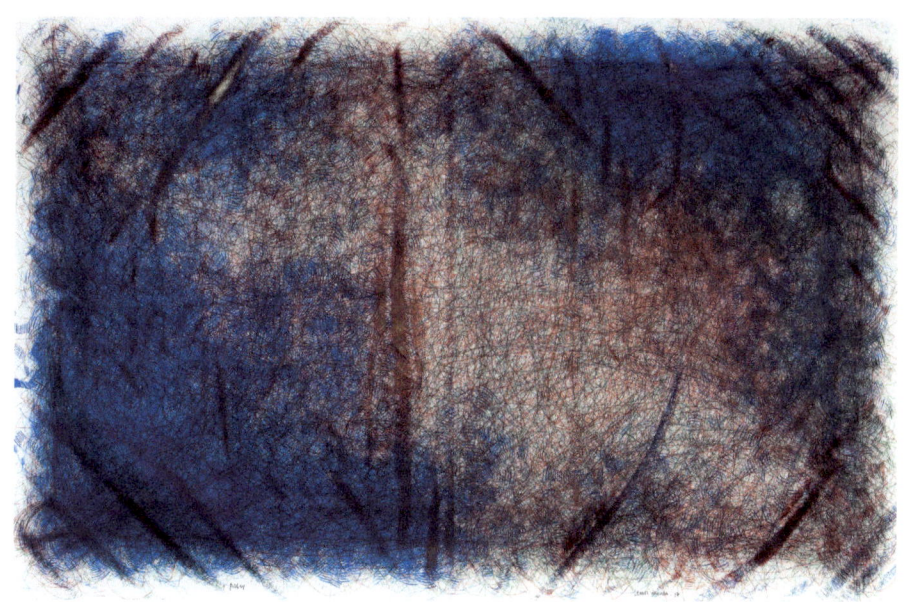

A060117, 2017, permanent ink on canvas PVC, 280 x 470 cm

A060217, 2017, permanent ink on canvas PVC, 280 x 470 cm

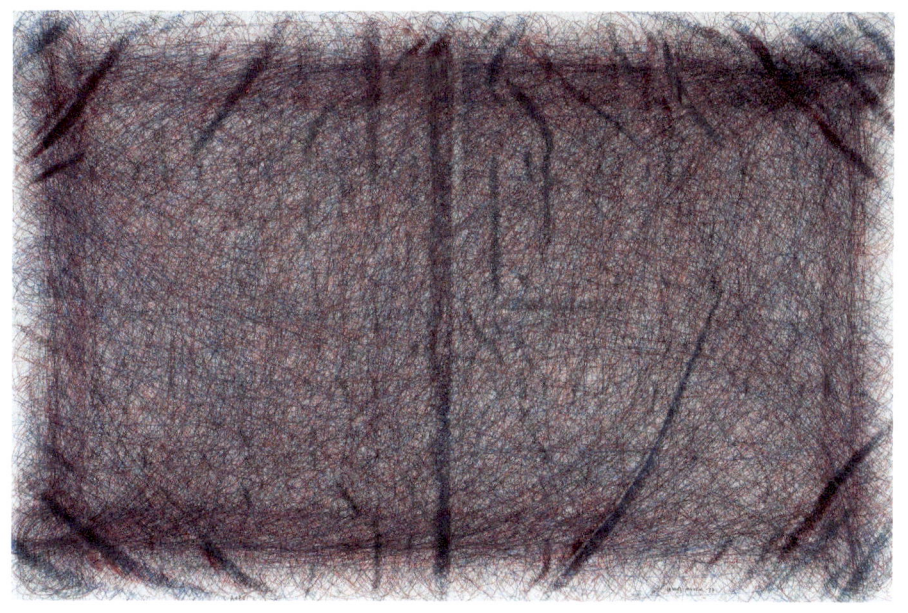

A070117, 2017, permanent ink on canvas PVC, 280 x 470 cm

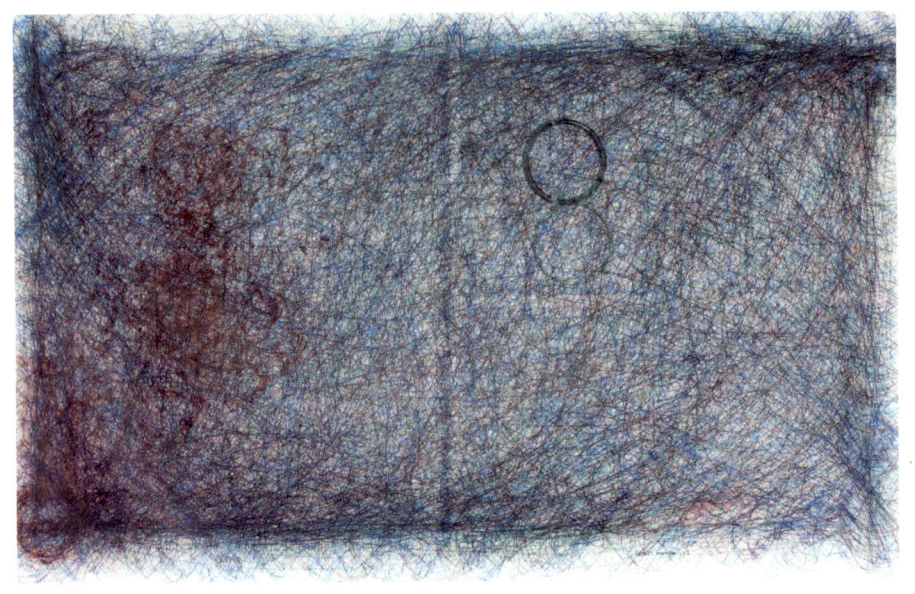

A070217, 2017, permanent ink on canvas PVC, 280 x 470 cm

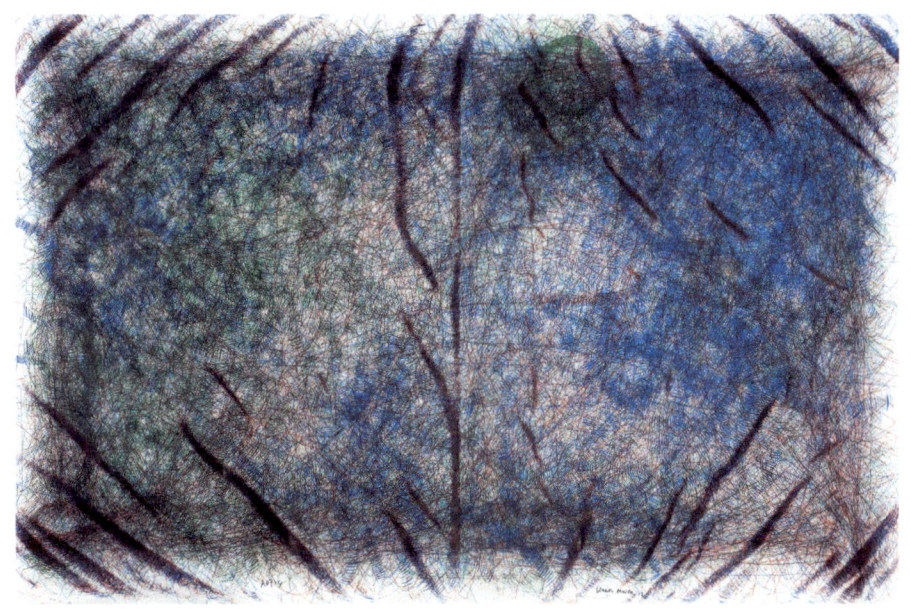

A070417, 2017, permanent ink on canvas PVC, 280 x 470 cm

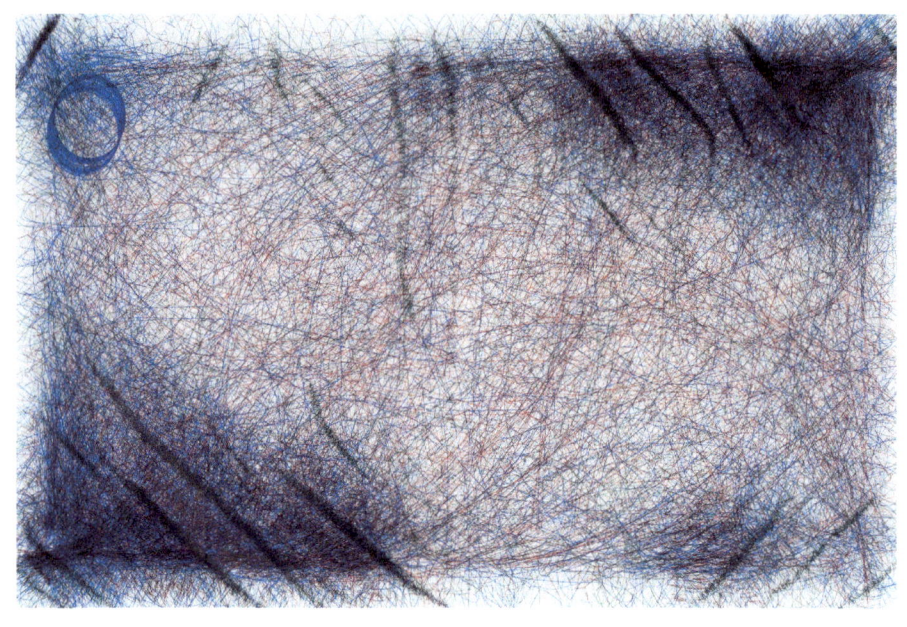

A070517, 2017, permanent ink on canvas PVC, 280 x 470 cm

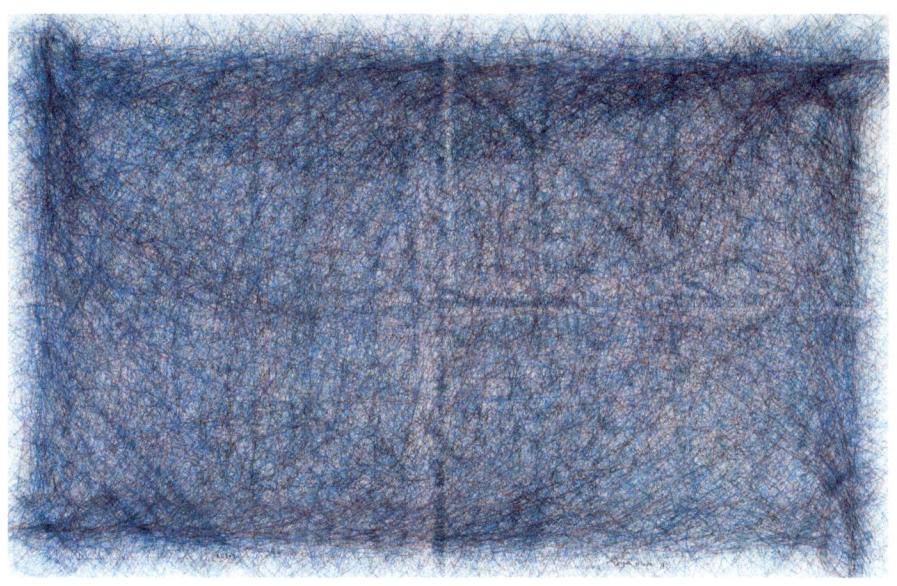

A080117, 2017, permanent ink on canvas PVC, 280 x 470 cm

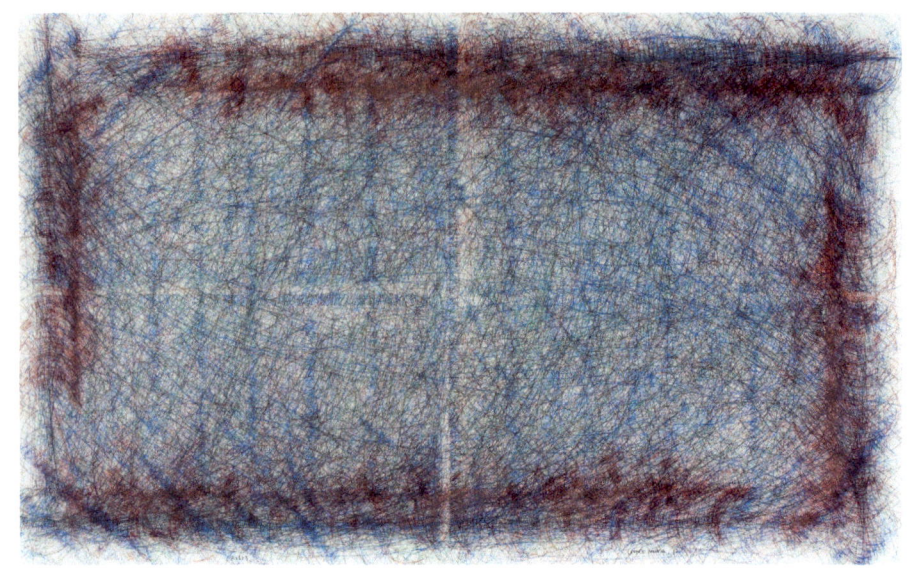

A080317, 2017, permanent ink on canvas PVC, 280 x 470 cm

LISBON
NOVEMBER | 2017

WEBSUMMIT

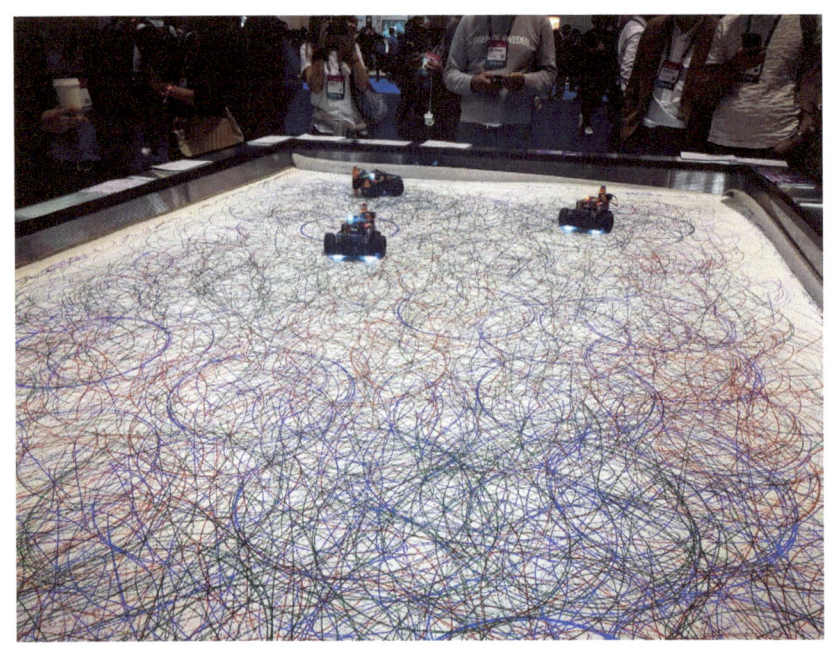

Working at the Websummit

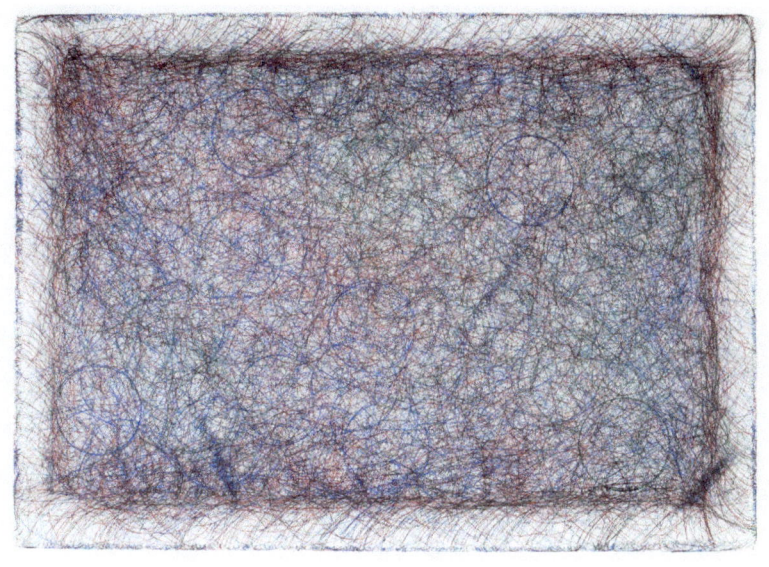

WS1, 2017, ink on canvas, 180 x 270 cm

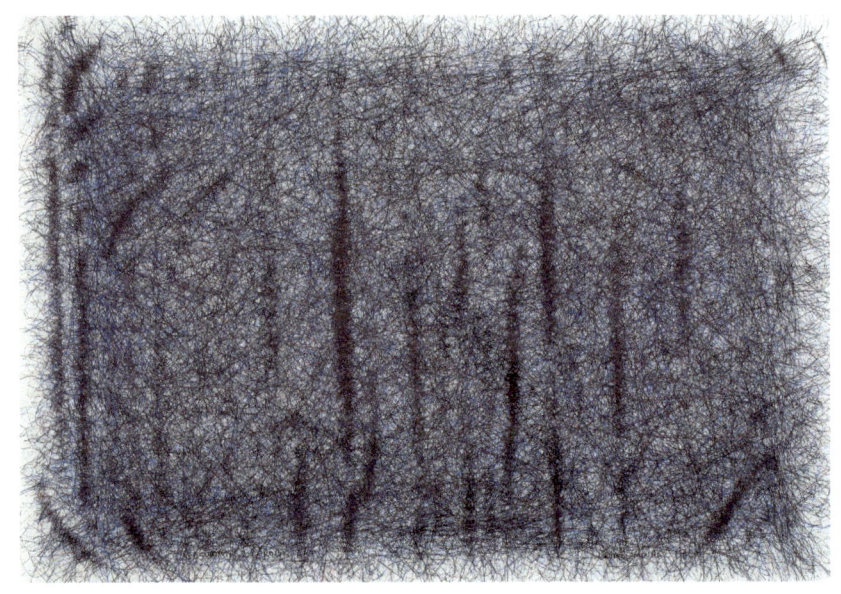

WS2, 2017, ink on canvas, 180 x 270 cm

PARIS

APRIL | JULY | 2018

GRAND PALAIS

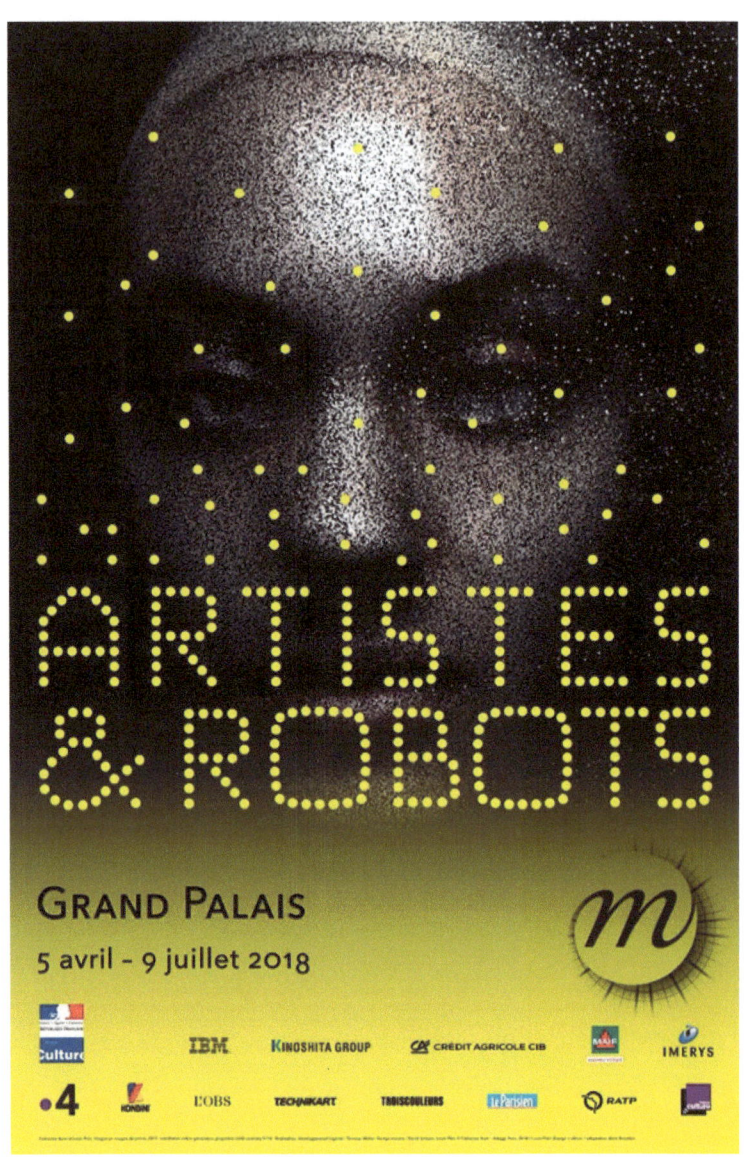

This exhibition is an opportunity to experience works of art produced with the help of increasingly sophisticated robots. Featuring works by some forty artists, it offers a gateway to an immersive and interactive digital world - an augmented body sensory experience that subverts our notions of space and time.

In an ever more robotic society, these artists explore new technologies, including Artificial Intelligence, which is potentially revolutionising human lives and even the conditions in which artworks are produced, presented, disseminated, conserved and received.

These works contain a warning. Although Artificial Intelligence can help us, it also threatens to make itself our master by reducing humans to simple slaves to performance.

Artists have extensive experience of this dangerous game: from the first prehistoric cave paintings, they have used technology to achieve a goal and then subjected it to their questions and imaginations.

Ever more sophisticated software has given rise to increasingly autonomous works, an ability to generate infinite forms, and interactivity with audiences who permanently modify this game.

[RMN | Grand Palais]

Artists: Jean Tinguely, Nam June Paik, Nicolas Schöffer, Leonel Moura, Patrick Tresset, So Kanno, Takahiro Yamaguchi, J. Lee Thompson, Arcangelo Sassolino, Manfred Mohr, Vera Molnar, Iannis Xenakis, Demian Conrad, Raquel Kogan, Ryoji Ikeda, Pascal Dombis, Elias Crespin, Jacopo Baboni Schilingi, Edmond Couchot and Michel Bret, Miguel Chevalier, Joan Fontcuberta, Michael Hansmeyer, Peter Kogler, Christa Sommerer and Laurent Mignonneau, Catherine Ikam and Louis Fléri, Stelarc, Nicolas Darrot, Fabien Giraud and Raphaël Siboni, Koji Fukada, Oscar Sharp, Daft Punk, Pascal Haudressy, Memo Akten, ORLAN, Takashi Murakami

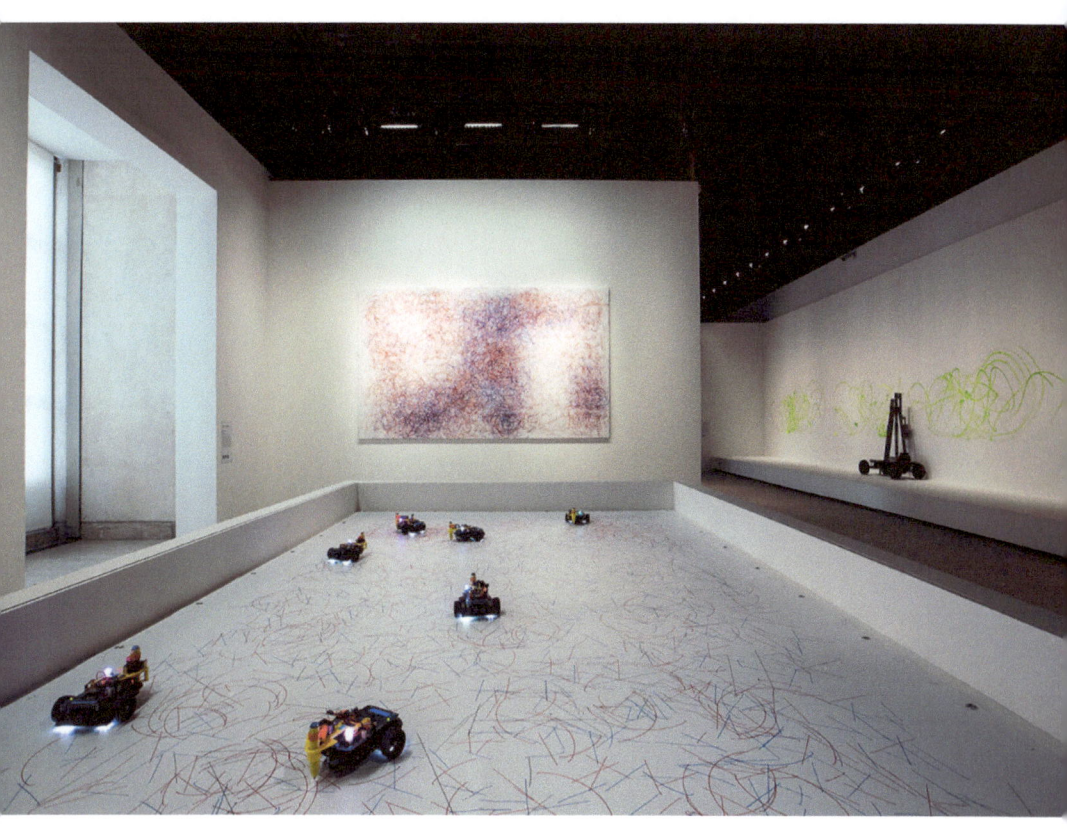

Grand Palais, installation view.

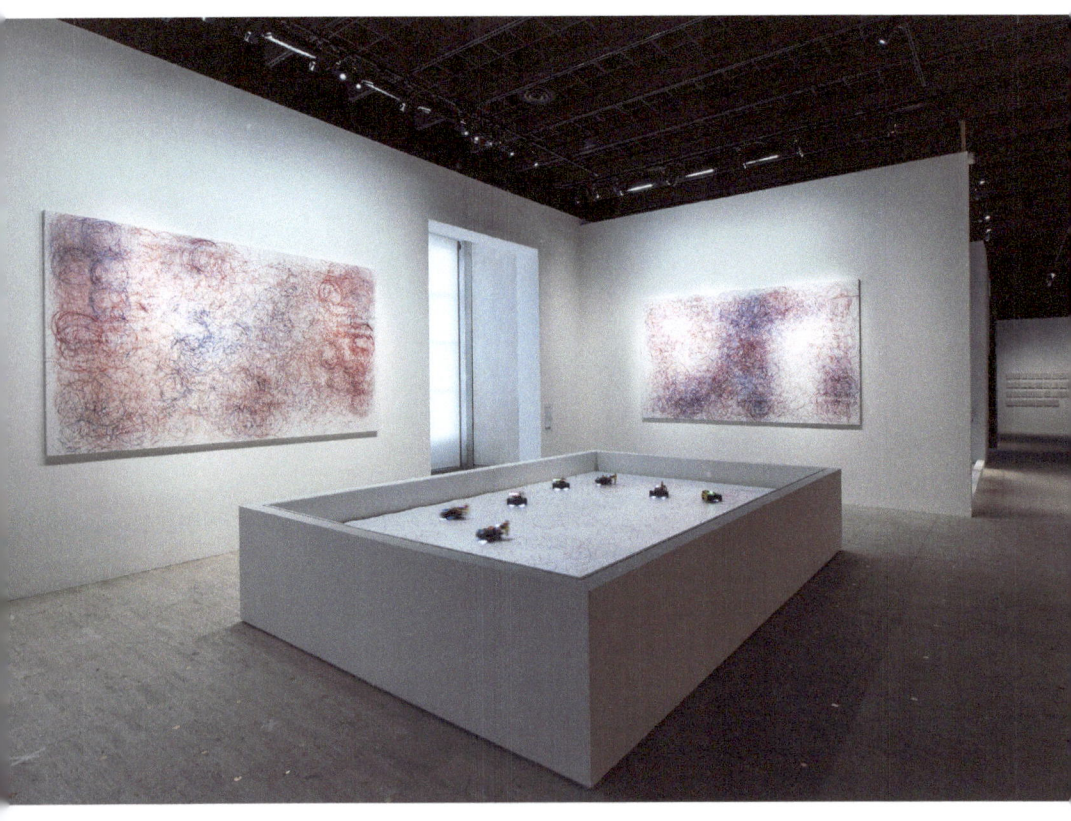

Grand Palais, installation view.

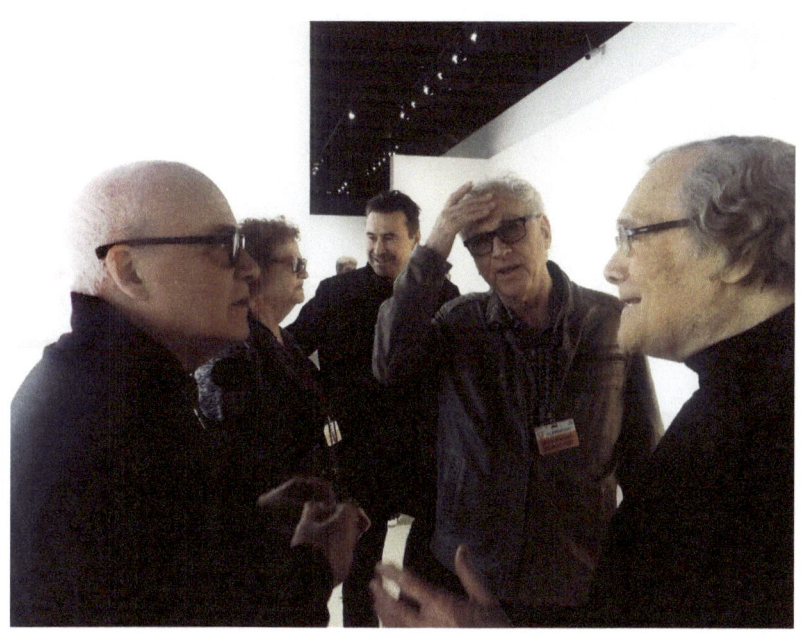

With Barbara Needle, Pascal Dombis, Manfred Mohr and Edmond Couchot

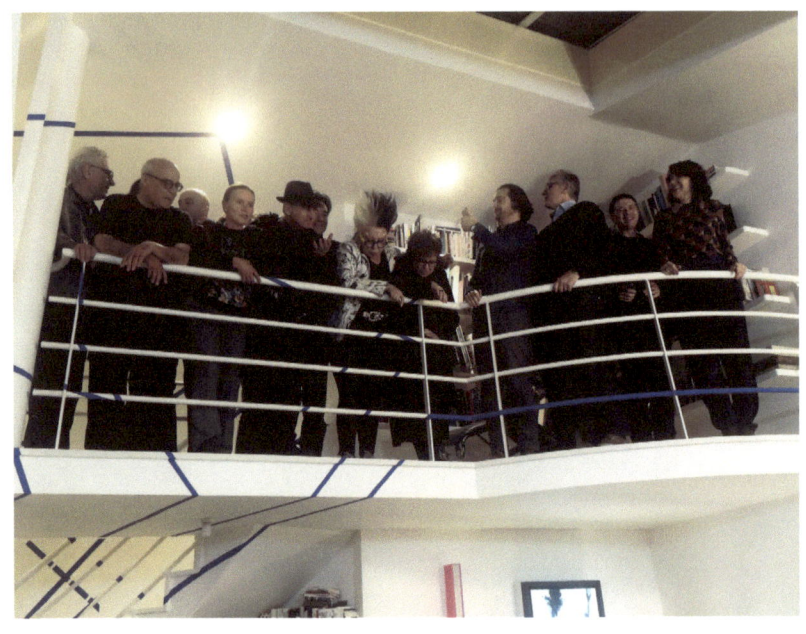

Artists at the balcony

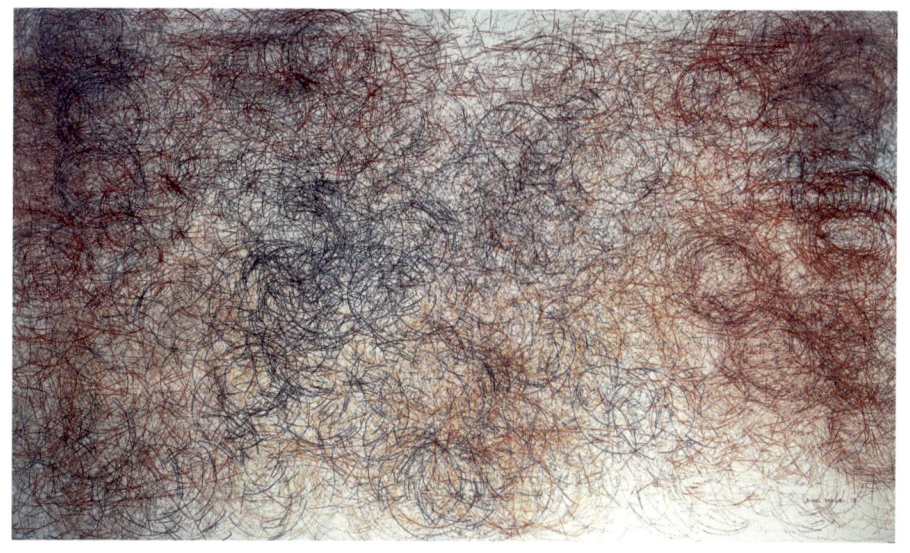

Bebot, Paris I, 2018, permanent ink on canvas, 208 x 355 cm

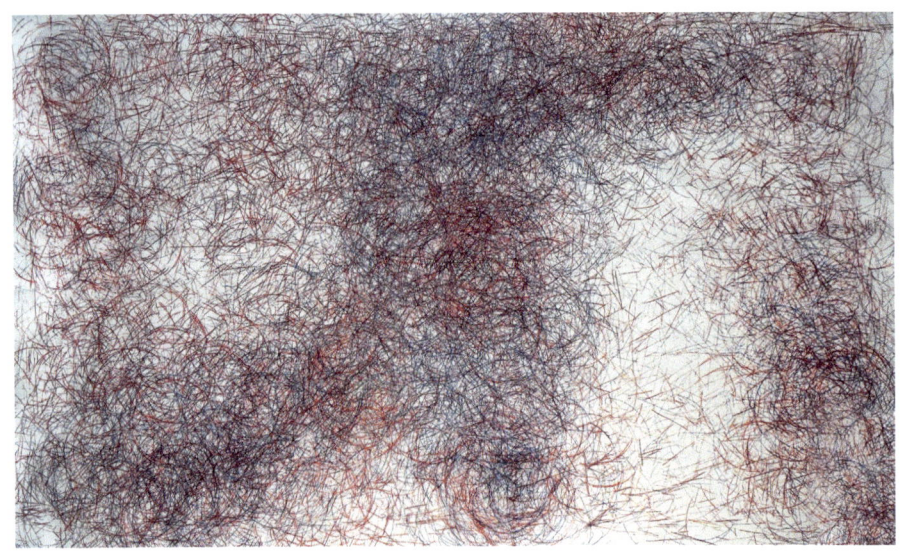

Bebot, Paris II, 2018, permanent ink on canvas, 208 x 355 cm

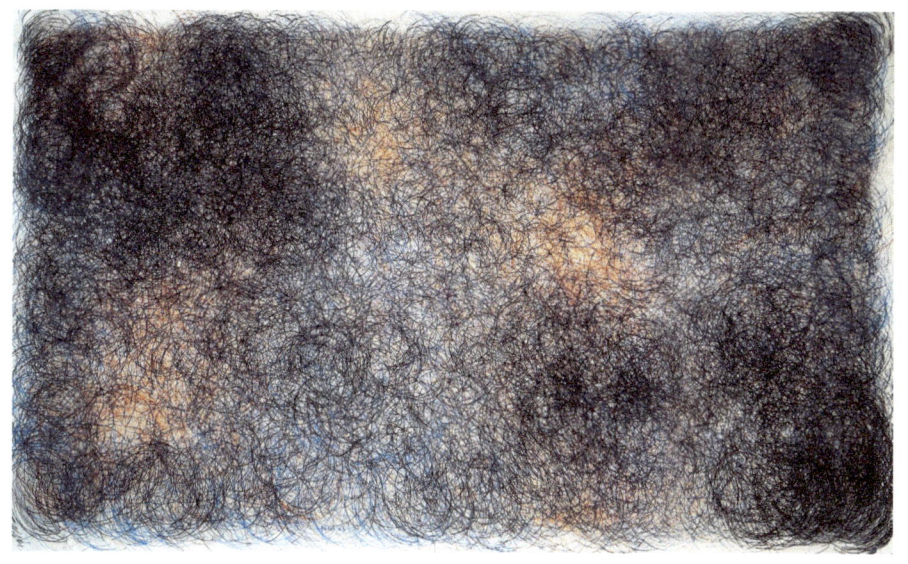

Bebot, Paris 03, 2018, permanent ink on canvas PVC, 280 x 470 cm

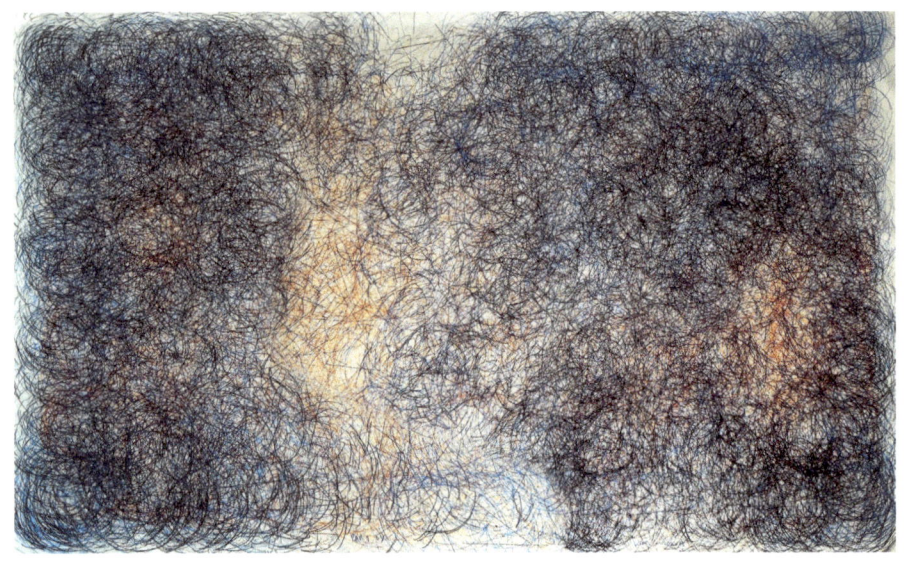

Bebot, Paris 04, 2018, permanent ink on canvas PVC, 280 x 470 cm

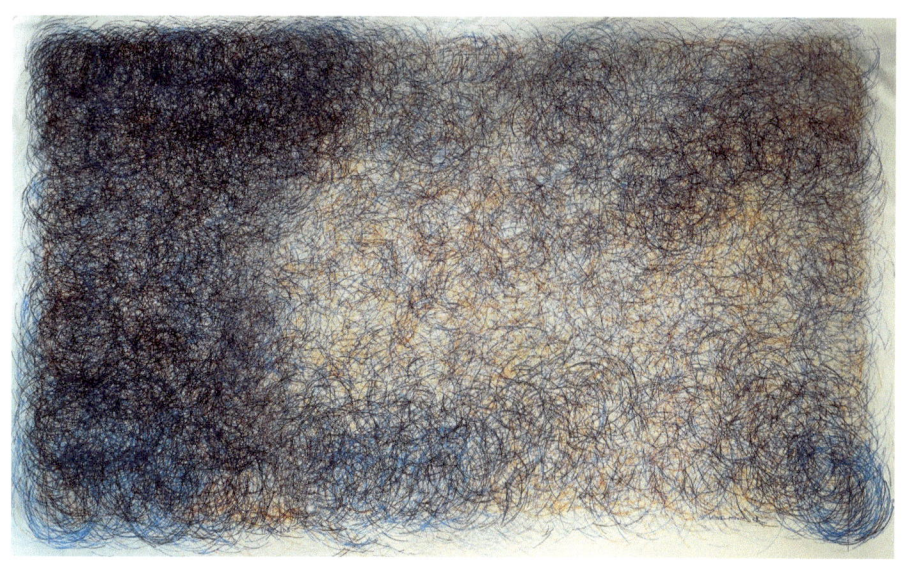

Bebot, Paris 05, 2018, permanent ink on canvas PVC, 280 x 470 cm

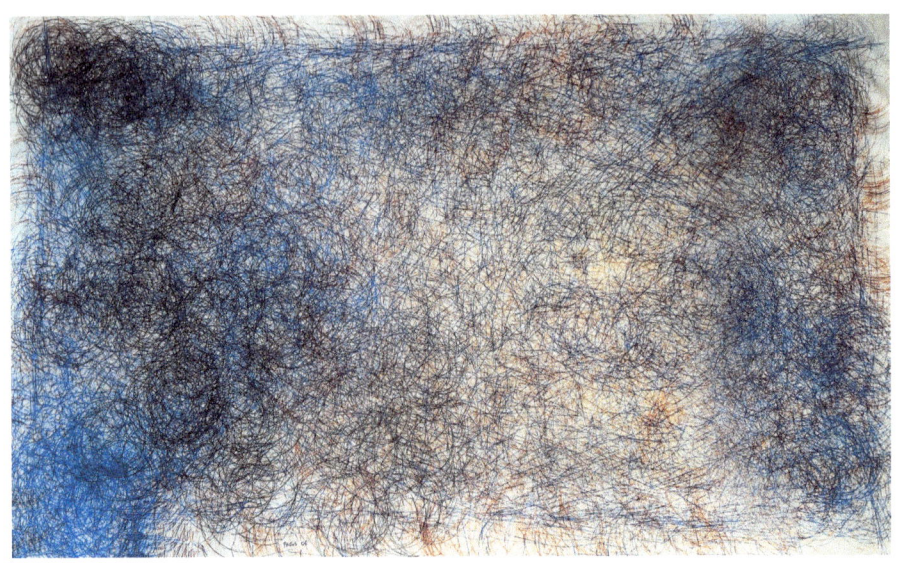

Bebot, Paris 06, 2018, permanent ink on canvas PVC, 280 x 470 cm

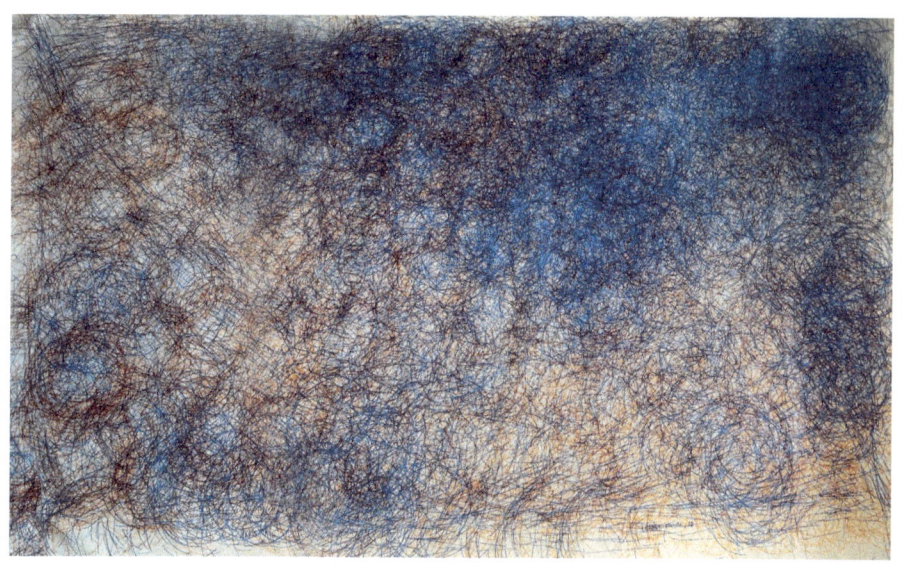

Bebot, Paris 07, 2018, permanent ink on canvas PVC, 280 x 470 cm

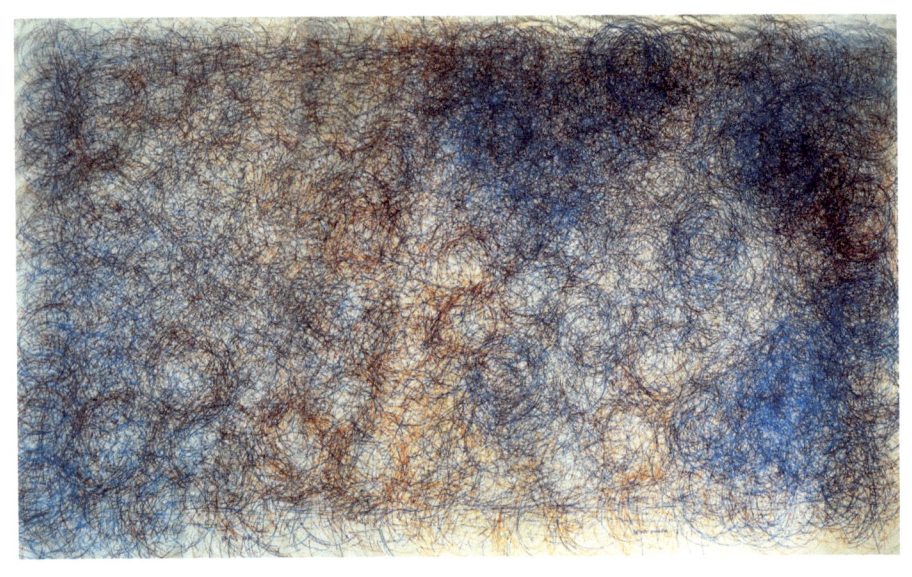

Bebot, Paris 08, 2018, permanent ink on canvas PVC, 280 x 470 cm

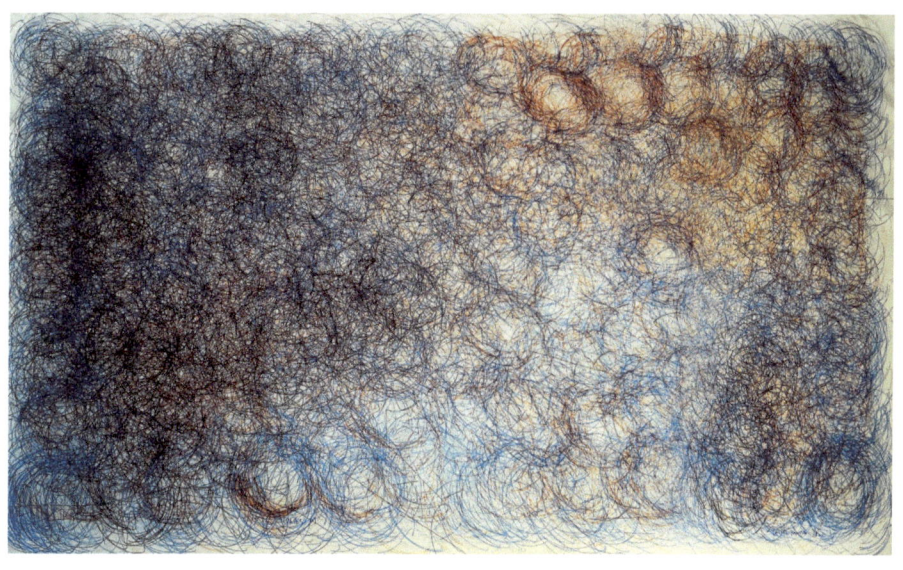

Bebot, Paris 09, 2018, permanent ink on canvas PVC, 280 x 470 cm

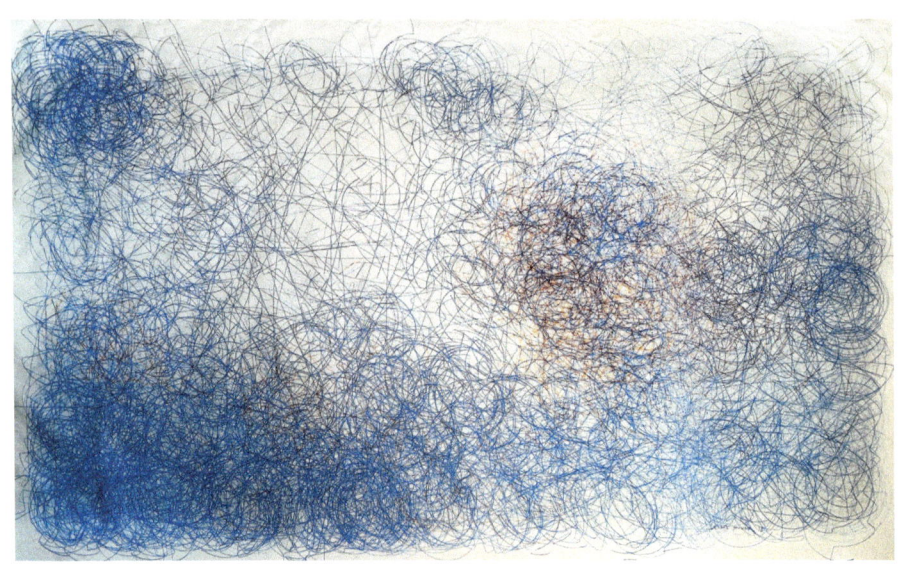

Bebot, Paris 10, 2018, permanent ink on canvas PVC, 280 x 470 cm

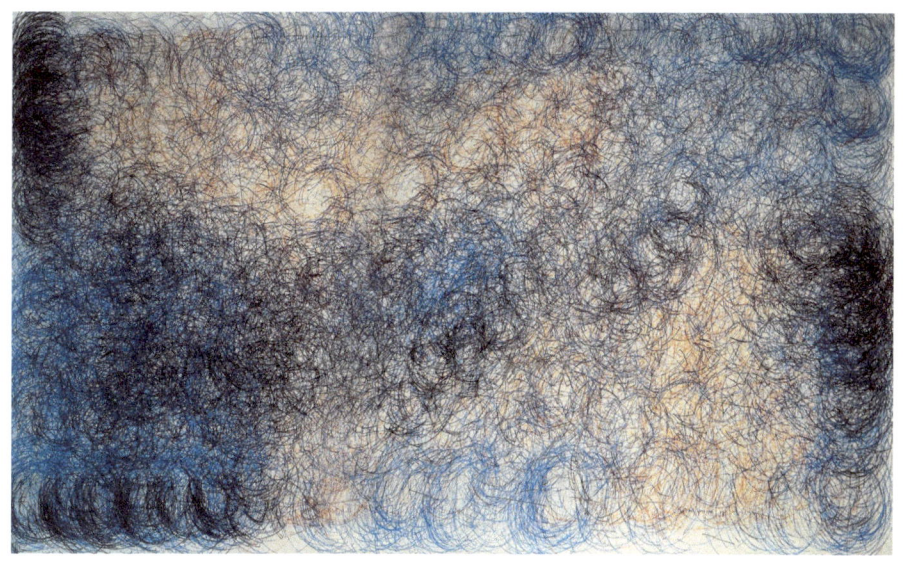

Bebot, Paris 11, 2018, permanent ink on canvas PVC, 280 x 470 cm

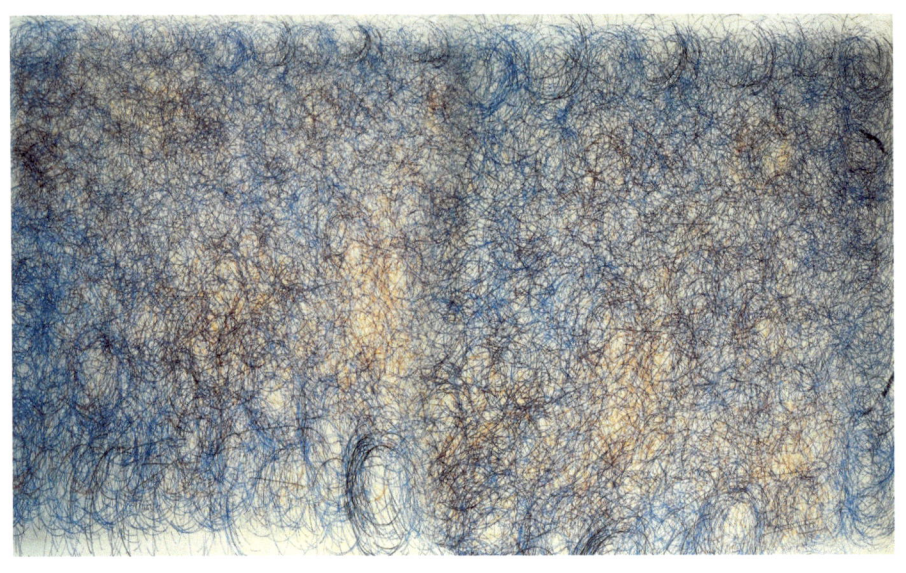

Bebot, Paris 12, 2018, permanent ink on canvas PVC, 280 x 470 cm

LISBON
MARS | JUNE | 2019

GULBENKIAN

Stigmergy Art

By the end of last century, I came across the concept of stigmergy. It was demonstrated by a new kind of bio-inspired algorithm created by Marco Dorigo in the early nineties, coined ACO (Ant Colony Optimization) also known as ant-algorithm. The algorithm simulates the behaviour of ants and termites and their particular form of indirect communication among individuals as described by Pierre-Paul Grassé, in studies that he carried out on social insects.

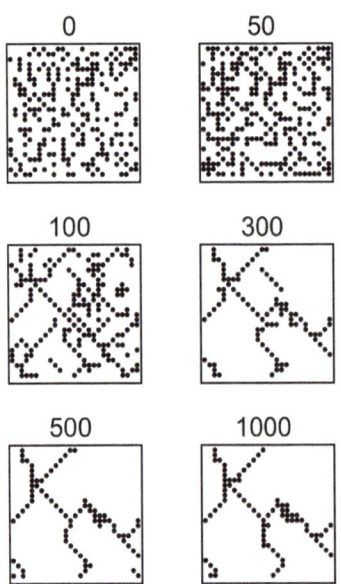

Fig. 1 Dorigo's ant algorithm: stigmergy at work.

When searching for food ants wander randomly, but upon finding it return to the colony while laying down a pheromone trail. If other ants come across such chemical path, they tend to halt the random wandering, and instead follow the trail reinforcing it. When the food is consumed ants stop adding pheromone and the trail vanishes.

Termites, which build remarkable clay constructions, are another example.

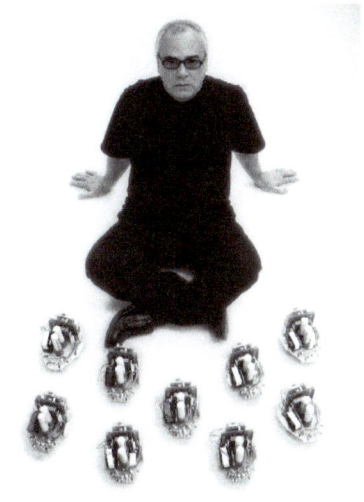

Fig. 2 A swarm of antlike robots. Photo LM studio.

At the start, the insects randomly deposit little balls of clay impregnated with pheromone. The formation of a pile stimulates other termites to add more clay, and the higher the piles, the greater the stimulus. Small mounds are abandoned. Some columns grow and come together until they touch, form¬ing arches. The result is an intricate and very solid structure.

Stigmergy (from stigma/sign and ergon/action) designates an indirect communication mechanism based on

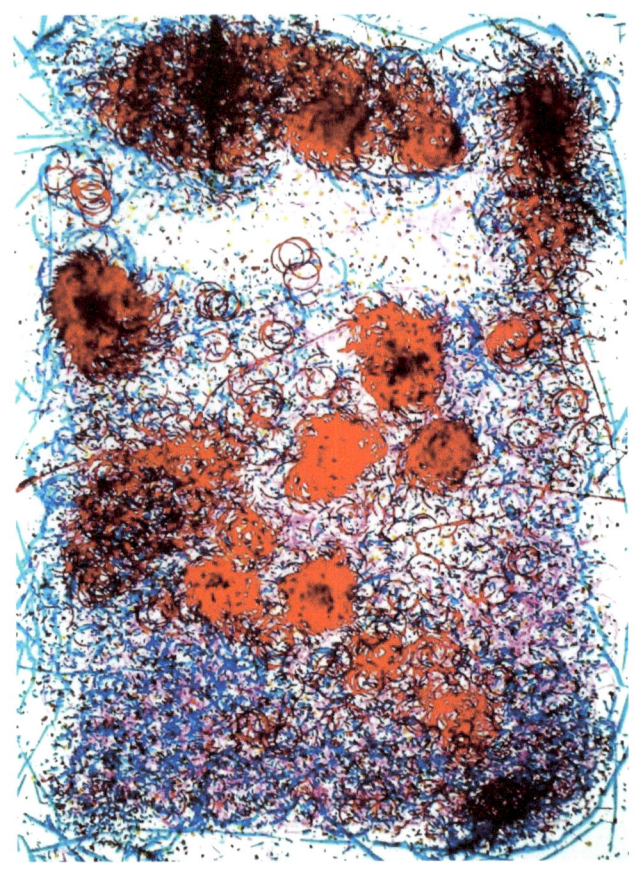

Fig.3 Artsbot 010304, 2004, ink on canvas, 195 x 130 cm. Photo LM studio.

signals left in the environment by one agent which trigger responses among other agents. It means that the coordination of tasks does not depend directly on the interactions between agents, but on the environment itself. The agent does not direct his work, but is guided by it.

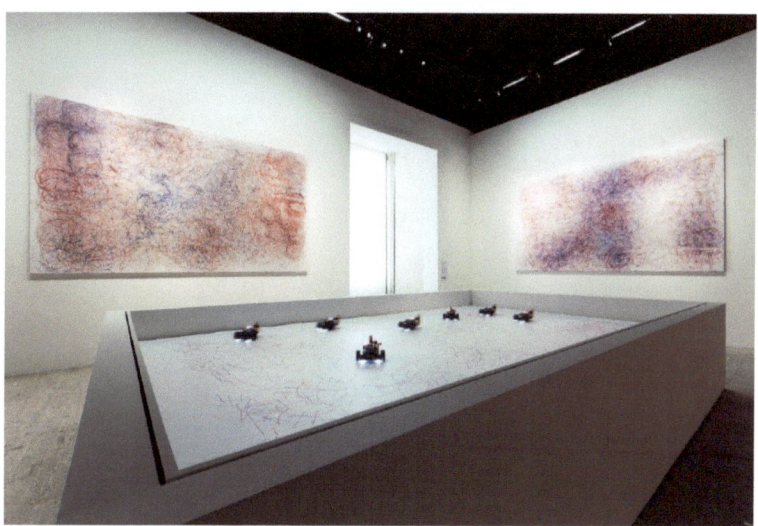

Fig. 4 Bebot Swarm, installation at Grand Palais, Paris, 2018. Photo Aldo Paredes, RMNGP.

Dorigo's first algorithm was apparently quite simple but it showed how from a chaotic random start a not predetermined order appears (Fig.1). Being an artist, I saw the emergence of self-organized drawings.

Following several experiments, in 2001 I switched from computer to robotics. Robots live in the real world, have sensors to detect obstacles and colour, and behave as a true swarm. I changed pheromone for colour. The art robots are stimulated by colour in the same way that ants are stimulate by pheromone. If they come across, they reinforce it.

Stimulus is a very important component in the stigmergy mechanism. Being machines dedicated to pictorial creations my robots are "excited" by colour.

Artsbot (Art Swarm Robots), produced in 2003 (Fig.2), demonstrate that when equipped with a set of simple rules based on stigmergy a swarm of robots can generate unique compositions independent from the human that starts the process. These antlike machines interact indirectly based on the colour traces that each one makes. The result of their actions is always unpredictable. Additionally, if randomness is an essential component of the process the resulting artwork cannot be described as random as organized patterns emerge from a fuzzy background. Actually, cluster formation is a demonstration that the process is not random (Fig. 3).

My art robots are performers that follow a choreography determined by stigmergy (Fig. 4). They walk around in a haphazard mode but when detect "their" colour, since each robot is stimulated by a specific colour, tend to reinforce it. And I say tend since the process is not 0 or 1. The algorithm uses tendencies rather than orders to simulate biological behaviour.

In artistic terms it is now possible to create art works without direct human intervention. The process is not random nor predetermined, but self-organized. Drawings that make itself. These art robots make art as ants make trails or termites makes clay cathedrals.

Considering the evolution of modern and contemporary art, which went from figurative to abstract, manufacture to ready-made, object to process, a self-organized form of art opens a new field of artistic exploration that objectively takes the human out of the loop. Hence, I coined it nonhuman art. This claim may be controversial in the context of mainstream art world which is essentially anthropocentric. But, actually, it is inscribed in the global evolution of robotics and artificial intelligence towards a greater autonomy of machines. Artificial intelligence will evolve to be more and more creative and less and less human dependent. Art announces what is about to come.

References
Beckers, R., Holland, O.E., Deneubourg, J.L. (1994) From local to global tasks: stigmergy and collective robotics, Artificial Life IV, Ed. R. Brooks, MIT

Bonabeau, E., Dorigo, M., Theraulaz, G. (1999) Swarm Intelligence, Oxford University Press

DeLanda M (2011) Philosophy and Simulation: The Emergence of Synthetic Reason, Continuum

Dennett, D (2009) The intentional stance, in Catalogue Inside art and science, LxXL

Grassé, P. P. (1959) La réconstruction du nid et les coordinations inter-individuelles chez Bellicositermes Natalienses et

cubitermes sp. La théorie de la stigmergie: Essai d'interprétation des termites constructeurs, Ins. Soc., 6, p. 41-48

Johnson, S (2001) Emergence: The Connected Lives of Ants, Brains, Cities, and Software, Scribner

Kelly, K (1994) Out of Control: The New Biology of Machines, Social Systems, and the Economic World, Basic Books

Langton, C. (1987) Proceedings of Artificial Life, Adison-Wesley

Moura, L. and Pereira, H.G. (2004) Symbiotic Art, Institut d'Art Contemporain, Collection Écrits d'artistes

Moura, L. (2016) Machines that make art, in Robots and Art, edited by Damith Herath, Christian Kroos, Stelarc, Springer

Shanken, E. (2001) Art in the information age: Technology and conceptual art, in Invisible College: Reconsidering

"Conceptual Art", Ed. Michael Corris, Cambridge UP

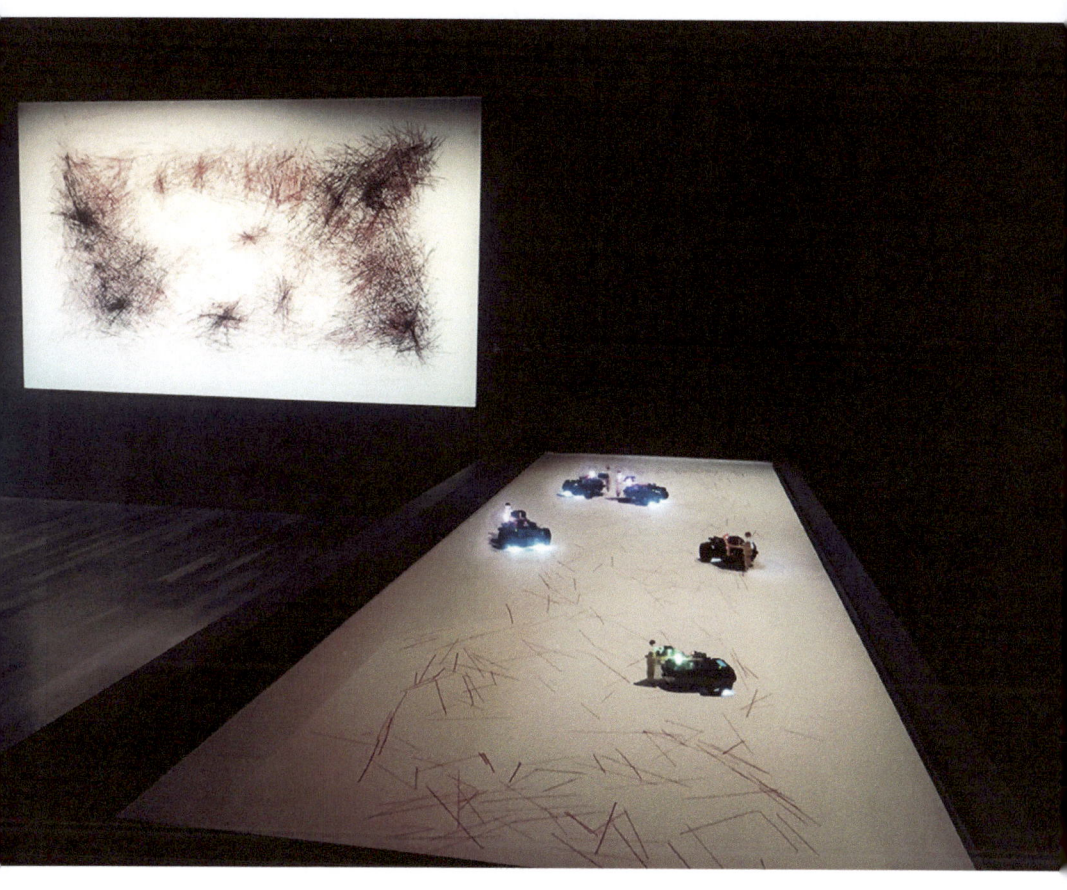

Installation view

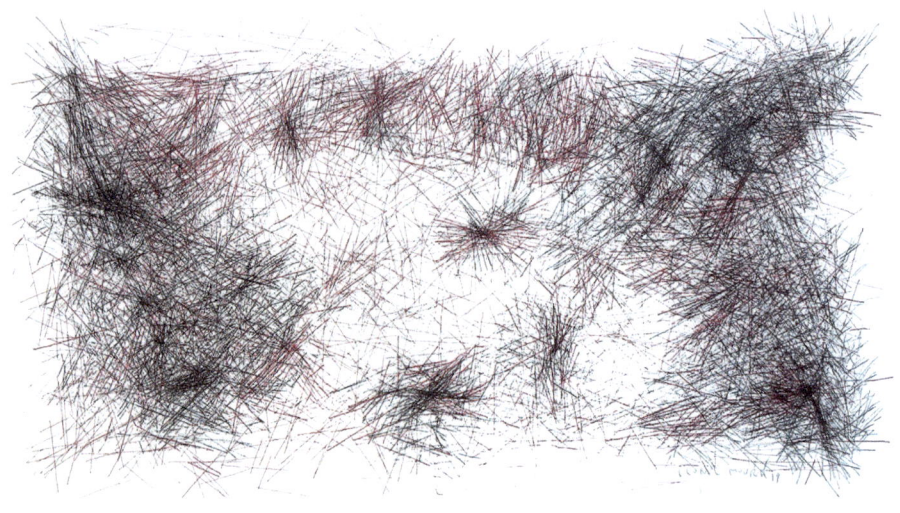

Bebot, Brain I, 2019, ink on canvas, 208 x 355 cm

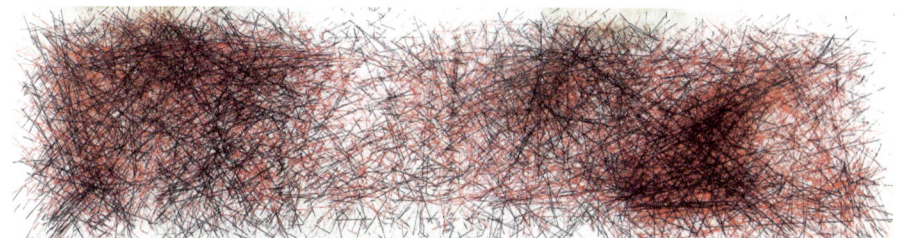

Brain II, 2019, ink on canvas, 120 x 450 cm

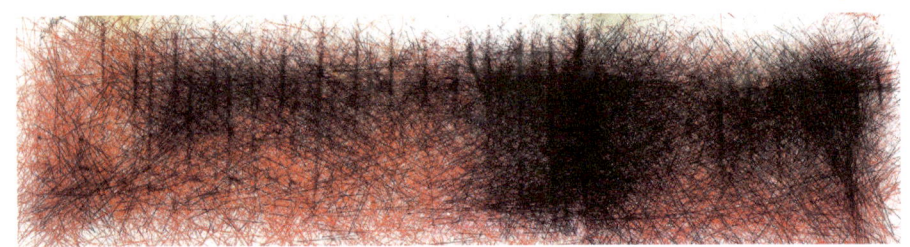

Brain III, 2019, ink on canvas, 120 x 450 cm

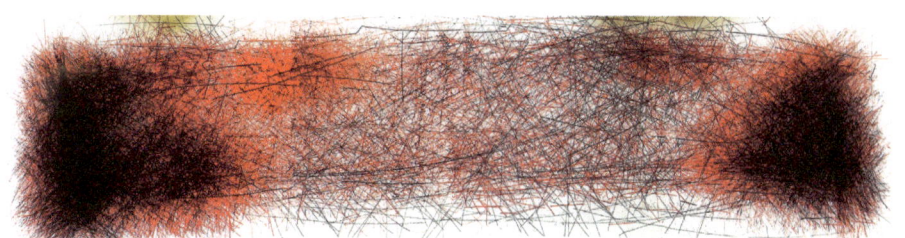

Brain IV, 2019, ink on canvas, 120 x 450 cm

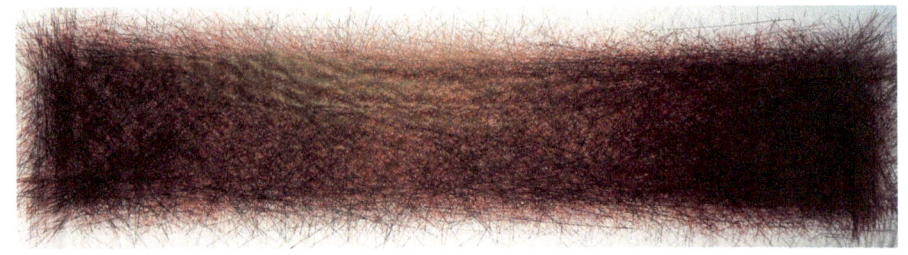

Brain V, 2019, ink on canvas, 120 x 450 cm

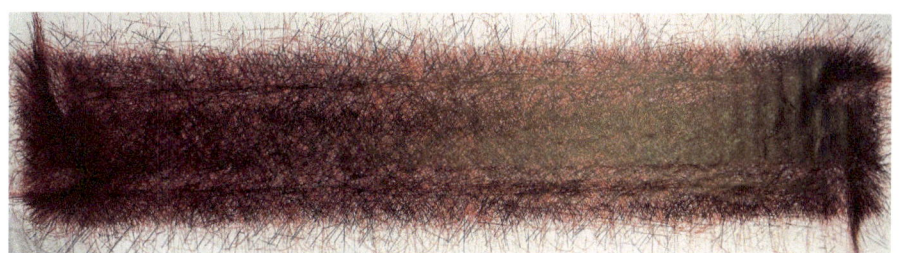

Brain VI, 2019, ink on canvas, 120 x 450 cm

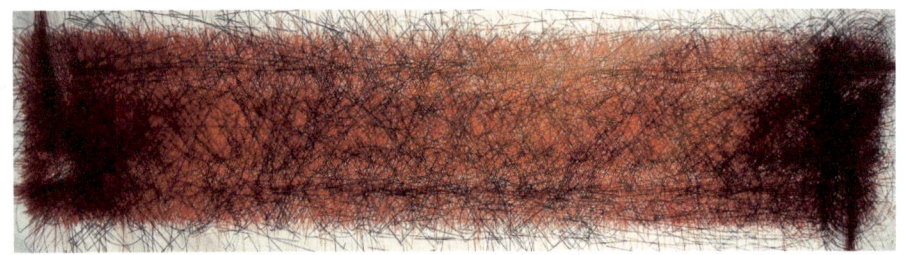

Brain VIII, 2019, ink on canvas, 120 x 450 cm

ÉCHARPE

2018

GRAND PALAIS BOUTIQUE

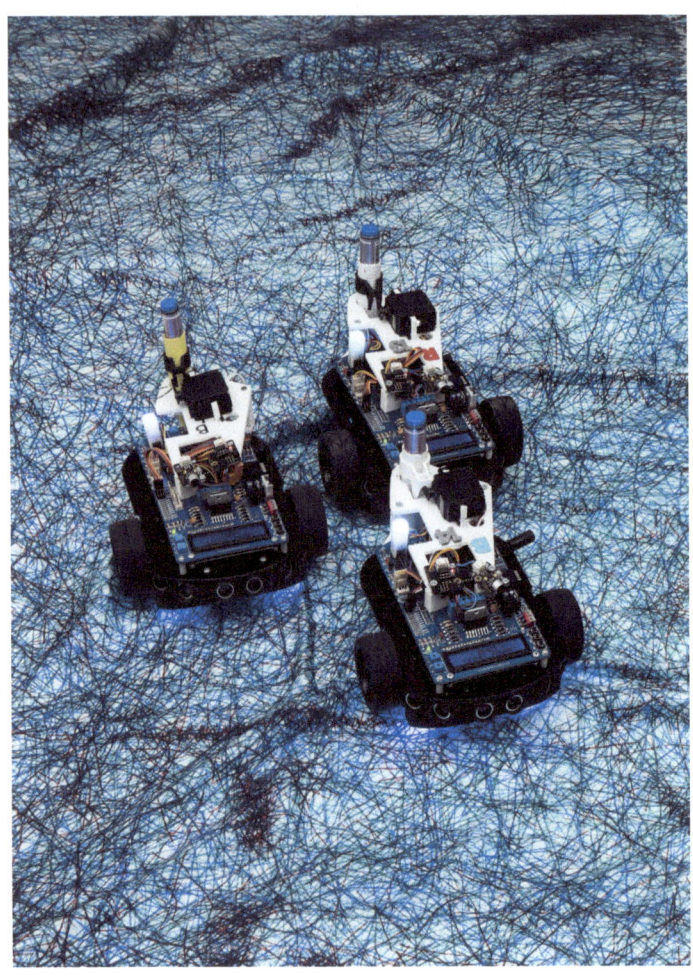

BeBot robots made the pattern for a 100% silk écharpe produced by the Boutique of Grand Palais.

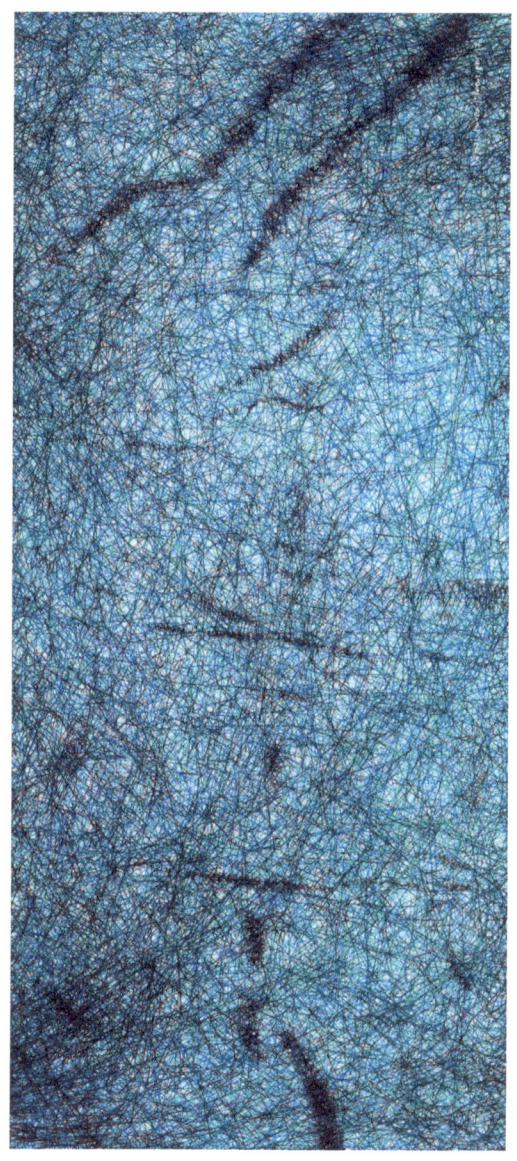

Silk, 80 x 200 cm.

BeBot list of works

Region	Year	Code	Medium	Size
Astana	2017	B020517	Ink on Canvas PVC	280 x 470
Astana	2017	B050517	Ink on Canvas PVC	280 x 470
Astana	2017	A0601	Ink on Canvas PVC	280 x 470
Astana	2017	A0602	Ink on Canvas PVC	280 x 470
Astana	2017	A0701	Ink on Canvas PVC	280 x 470
Astana	2017	A0702	Ink on Canvas PVC	280 x 470
Astana	2017	A0704	Ink on Canvas PVC	280 x 470
Astana	2017	A0705	Ink on Canvas PVC	280 x 470
Astana	2017	A0801	Ink on Canvas PVC	280 x 470
Astana	2017	A0803	Ink on Canvas PVC	280 x 470
Astana	2017	A0804	Ink on Canvas PVC	280 x 470
Websummit	2017	WS1	Ink on canvas	180 x 270
Websummit	2017	WS2	Ink on canvas	180 x 270
Paris	2018	Paris I	Ink on canvas	208 x 355
Paris	2018	Paris II	Ink on canvas	208 x 355
Paris	2018	Paris 03	Ink on Canvas PVC	280 x 470
Paris	2018	Paris 04	Ink on Canvas PVC	280 x 470
Paris	2018	Paris 05	Ink on Canvas PVC	280 x 470
Paris	2018	Paris 06	Ink on Canvas PVC	280 x 470
Paris	2018	Paris 07	Ink on Canvas PVC	280 x 470
Paris	2018	Paris 08	Ink on Canvas PVC	280 x 470
Paris	2018	Paris 09	Ink on Canvas PVC	280 x 470
Paris	2018	Paris 10	Ink on Canvas PVC	280 x 470
Paris	2018	Paris 11	Ink on Canvas PVC	280 x 470
Paris	2018	Paris 12	Ink on Canvas PVC	280 x 470
Lisbon	2018	B070118	Ink on canvas	160 x170
Lisbon	2019	Brain I	Ink on canvas	208 x 355
Lisbon	2019	Brain II	Ink on canvas	120 x 450
Lisbon	2019	Brain III	Ink on canvas	120 x 450
Lisbon	2019	Brain IV	Ink on canvas	120 x 450
Lisbon	2019	Brain V	Ink on canvas	120 x 450
Lisbon	2019	Brain VI	Ink on canvas	120 x 450
Lisbon	2019	Brain VII	Ink on canvas	120 x 450
Lisbon	2019	Brain VIII	Ink on canvas	120 x 450

www.ingramcontent.com/pod-product-compliance
Lightning Source LLC
Chambersburg PA
CBHW041941240526
45473CB00033B/167